Short Poems for a Long and Happy Life

Karla Mosley

Published by
RockStar Publishing House
32129 Lindero Canyon Road, Suite 205
Westlake Village, CA 91361
www.rockstarpublishinghouse.com

Copyright © 2014 by Karla Mosley

All rights reserved. No part of this book may be reproduced or transmitted in any form or by in any means, electronic or mechanical, including photocopying, recording, or by any information storage and retrieval system, without the written permission of the Publisher, except where permitted by law.

Manufactured in the United States of America, or in the United Kingdom when distributed elsewhere.

Mosley, Karen
   Short Poems for a Long and Happy Life
   ISBN:
   Paperback: 9781937506780
   eBook: 9781937506797

Cover design by: Michael Short
Cover photo courtesy Shutterstock.com
Interior design: Scribe Inc.
Photo credits: Photographer name(s)
Permission credits: If any

http://karlamosley.com/

For my muses.

Two years ago I read an article about a man in Japan who was over 100 years old and had been writing a Haiku every day for over 50 years.

Inspired by him, I began to write and eventually publicly committed myself to write one haiku a day for a year. It became the "Haiku Project 2012". And I did it...for the most part. Like a good child of the digital age I cheated by taking off a few days and then binge writing to make up for the lost time. But I still say it counts (that's the nice thing about being the creator, participant and judge of a competition built for one).

I also recently learned that most of my poems are not Haikus at all, but Senyus or some other form of micro poetry (a Haiku historically involves nature - but I'm probably much too urban for that on a daily basis. As much as I try to see the forest for the trees, it is much less inspiring when you are staring at the same tree surrounded by a few mangy blades of dog poop encrusted grass in a planter outside your window. But I digress).

Anyhow, I was posting my poetry on various social media sites when people began asking for a book of these musings. At first I thanked these apparently simple minded people and chuckled to myself, "Who would want a book of my brain drain?" But as I started receiving inquiries from different people every day, I had to take a look at who was being small minded, "Who wouldn't want a book of my brain drain? I could be the next Shel Silverstein!" And then I had to stick a pin in my over-inflated ego and come back down to earth, "Let's just give it a try".

A little over two years after finishing Haiku Project 2012, I am publishing my first book of poetry. My husband, the lawyer, would have me include the disclaimer that I can in no way guarantee that these poems will ensure that you will celebrate a century's worth of birthdays or that it will prevent any other personal or global apocalypses. But I do hope you enjoy reading them as I have enjoyed writing them and re-discovering them through the creation of this book. This project has been a wonderful personal adventure and I thank you deeply for your support.

-Karla

Contents

Preface v

Good Morning 2

Nature – True Haikus 4

Revolution 10

she/he/she 16

Love & Longing 22

Love.Self.Care 30

Remembering 34

Life Lessons 40

Friends, Family, Home 50

Joy & The Real Deal 54

Spark of Creation – An Artist's Dilemma 62

Letting Go 68

Ode 74

Prayer 78

Good Night 82

Epilogue 86

Acknowledgements 89

Good Morning

1 The morning buzzard
    Shakes me from a deep slumber
    Night gives birth to light

2 Early morning hush
    Before information clouds -
    Pure, Simple, Divine

3 Little kitty paws
    Descending like Storm Troopers
    Demanding Breakfast

4 Good morning panic,
    My dear old friend, whose bear hugs
    Remind me I care

5 Cozy Sunday morn.
    Hot mug, a worn book, pillows...
    Don't think I'll leave bed

Nature – True Haikus

6   Like my wise old cat
    I soak sun in through windows
    Waiting for my mouse

7   "Winter"
    Full moon in Harlem
    Spotlight on frozen fist pounds
    This corner's bumpin'

8   Wet, grey mountain fog
    Whose opaque clouds steal my sight
    So I must find feet

9   In frigid weather
    Some revel in icy dark
    I look for the sun

10 Sun, bringing new life,
    Warm my wintry, wind-chapped face
    And let my soul shine

11 "Shine On"
    Cue the hopeful sun
    Who knows that one day we will
    Look into her eyes

12 "Hope"
    From somewhere unknown
    A patch of blue, still miles off,
    Was heading this way

13 Without the darkness
    I might never know how great
    It feels to sunbathe

14 Shocking golden rays
    Pierce through blue-grey cloud's blankets
    Heaven Graze Green Earth

15 There's no stopping it
    Once a seed has been planted
    We must let it grow

16 City noise, please stop!
    Cars, cell phone & siren's song -
    Give way to bird's calls

17 In simplicity's
    Grassy plains & clear blue skies
    I've refound my joy

18 "Walk of Shame"
    Solemn slugs parade
    Across a soggy sidewalk
    Back to grassy home

19 The earth never stops
    She grows even as I rest
    And rocks me to sleep.

20 "Retrograde"
    Since Hermes' Moonwalk
    My gaze has moved - outside in
    The world - upside down

21 Moonshine so brightly
    The oft blueblack sky's ablaze
    Nighttime solar rays

22 Past sleepy twilight
    Loud trumpets of brazen dawn
    March across the sky

23 Rising with the sun
Pond'ring what the day might bring
Open to it all.

24 I wonder if fish
Are as happy in a bowl
As they'd be at sea

25 Sweaty summer night
Sticky bodies lay waiting
For the storm to break

26 Ominous quiet
Pea green sky before the storm
Black clouds, poised to weep

27 First storm of summer.
Thunder crash, my orchestra;
Cinematic flash

28 Satisfying sting
Of salt water scouring
Life's little lesions

29 Butterflies play
As we ride the waves of life
Into paradise

30 This human engine
    Doesn't roar from cars & trains
    It beats from within

31 I'll miss you crickets
    When I'm gone – serenade me
    With your country song

32 Autumn Harvest.
    Watch jigsaw puzzle actions craft
    The year's masterpiece.

33 From sweet, red apples
    To the bitterest of greens
    Nature serves us best

34 3 colors, 1 tree
    And, likewise, TRUE love can hold
    All the shades of me

35 Even in stillness
    The in out woosh of blood moves
    We're only vessels

36 If the sun can rise
    Every morning to give light,
    I can rise today

Revolution

37 She chooses thin ice
      For roads tread by the masses
      Buckle beneath her

38 A passing something
      Shining possibility
      And I Stand. Grounded.

39 Womanly assets
      Once, by media, made foes
      Now make me feel whole

40 White, billowy clouds
      Over tenement buildings
      Dreaming in concrete

41 Hatred only thrives
      Behind a wall of fear
      There are no strangers

42 What if we didn't
    Run down the same dull pathways?
    Some day I'll turn left…

43 When the edge was near
    And the brain was screaming "Quit!!"
    The bird learned to fly

44 Tempting as yours looks
    My feet are fixed firmly on
    The path I've chosen

45 It's perseverance
    Through resistance that creates
    Transformation

46 The fountain of youth
    Lies in service to others
    Beauty – inside out

47 I could rest easy
    Once I knew that my neighbors
    Were dreamers like me

48 A rounding tummy
    Skin worn from years of sun
    This body celebrates life

49 Though aging, it seems
    I find greater pools of tears
    With each passing year

50 This rugged pathway
    Has turned my feet from puss sores
    To calloused wisdom

51 There's no time like now
    To release your wintry hate
    And let love warm you

52 "Mirror, Mirror…"
    Funhouse gags
    Won't work on me
    Beauty's what I see

53 I fear little more
    Than the unfamiliar gaze
    Of passing strangers

54 I was shocked to find
     My enemy's reflection
     Is the same as mine

55 When battles are won
     In a war not worth fighting
     Triumph reeks of loss

56 Finding more patience
     For the things I resist most
     Discomfort yields peace

57 The loud tick tock clock
     From deep slumber once roused me
     Now it marks my step

58 In every city
     Hard work, families and love
     Common ground abounds

59 Great adversity
     Is like the rain cloud, which cries
     To make flowers grow

60 Months of wound so tight
    It's become my new normal
    Now letting go hurts

61 Taking the edge off.
    Fleshy thighs and Newborn hips
    Humanhood embraced

62 Won't you like me if
    I twist turn pretzel myself?
    Please hurt me some more

63 Dirt under thumbnail
    You elusive particle
    Out my subtle quirks

64 Grounded in center
    Arms reaching wide to balance
    Life's light and dark sides

65 If you knew for sure
    That it would all be ok
    What would you let go?

she/he/she

66 When these travelers met
      They knew their journey would span
      The rest of their lives

67 How long had they been
      Composing the same story?
      Lifetimes, I suppose.

68 She loved his quirks most
      The way his rough edges chafed
      Against her smooth bits

69 He loved her obstinance
      Particularly when
      She knew she was wrong

70 Sometimes honesty
      Could feel like a burden
      He'd rather not carry

71 Despite gravity
    She was often found flying
    Laughing at the ground

72 Sometimes a big Yes
    Sunk its claws deep in his heart
    But No still prevailed

73 Attempting to dodge exhaustion,
    She was oft found
    Asleep on the floor

74 At once he realized
    That the consequence of "Yes"
    Will always be change…

75 Heat soaked, sweating sheets
    She anticipates, short breathed,
    Her lover's return

76 Fingernails clutch cloth
    Collarbones reach; heart expands
    His tremors release

77 Had they swapped out hearts?
    The theft of his was certain
    Replacement – unsure

78 In the dark corner
    Of her well hid feeling chest
    Sat melancholy

79 In night's radio
    Silence festered a longing
    She'd never reveal

80 Internal unrest
    Had settled in her stomach
    A rot for truth's salve

81 Though her dreams
    Were almost like real life
    She still wished to live in that world

82 He'd cut that part out. Dreams.
    Set it in a locked box
    And let go of sleep

83 Broken commitments
    Sticky heart-un-felt sorrys
    And awkward breakfasts

84 One day he stood still
    And years of squashed emotions
    Dropped him to his knees

85 Waves of deep regret
    Swept the ocean of her face
    How'd we drift so far?

86 "I'm not yours," he said.
    And through two ironclad fists
    She slowly let go.

87 Once alone at last
    She couldn't help but long for
    What she'd pushed away

88 With no defenses
    His umbrella lost to squall
    He found soggy strength

89 Surrounded by space
     Expansive quiet and breath
     He felt his heartbeat

90 They sat and listened
     Because it's what they needed
     Virtue over Love

91 Once the wreckage clears
     He must step into the light
     Or die a relic

92 And although she thought
     She was the teacher, she learns.
     Student once again…

93 In between knowing
     Weightless, bodiless, spaceless
     Now dis-illusioned

94 Bump Crash Thrash Collide
     Relief erupts from inside
     Steep hill, now their slide

Love & Longing

95 If love grew on trees
     I would pick the ripest fruit
     And give it to you

96 "Midnight Valentine"
     I thought myself safe
     Then from nowhere you appeared
     And I am undone

97 Our last few moments
     Oceanside, open mouth snore
     Bliss-cicles now melt

98 "Recovered Fondness"
     In the deafening
     Din of solitude I see
     How much I love you

99 I'd said my good-byes
     But with siren's song she calls
     Bidding me to stay

100 Our connection quest -
     A series of wonderf'ly
     Failed almost moments

101 I'm missing something
     I never had. But my heart
     Aches as if I did.

102 This poor heart would break
     Should I show you all of me
     And watch you retreat

103 Old wounds re-opened
     Summer heat seeps deep inside
     Like salt to raw skin

104 From oceans away
     You're insides are my insides
     Your breaking heart, mine.

105 I had one nerve
     But you tangoed on it so
     Now I'm off to bed

106 Unable to stop
     My determined synapses
     From firing you up

107 You must be brilliant
Because our conversations
In my head are great…

108 "Commuter Love"
Your morning kisses
Shared by this beige subway crowd
Turned nude moods neon

109 My extremities
Long for your skilled knee joints
To thaw icy toes

110 Somehow in a crowd
Loneliness found it's way in
And asked me to dance

111 Crashing, arms thrashing
Gasping for breath and laughing
Caught in your riptide

112 Your contradictions
Stay lingering in my mind
Leave me still. Breathless.

113 With no booze consumed
      This hangover is intense…
      Love can wear you out.

114 Your breath – the sea's sigh
      Sunlight rising in your eyes
      Quick kiss…time to fly

115 "Silent Love"
      Lying beside me
      No words are necessary –
      Your foot on my thigh

116 I can see
      Beauty better through
      Your glasses

117 If I could only
      Believe in myself as much
      As you say you do

118 The gaps between us
      Make me love you even more
      Now than before

119 I could have long stayed
      Gazing deeply into you
      But you quickly blinked

120 Face pressed up against
      The ice wall surrounding you
      Longing for your warmth

121 Buoyed by nothing
      Groundlessness has its way as
      We dance with the fates

122 You. Cranky as hell.
      Me. Sweat and porcupine stubble.
      Here's to busted love.

123 Long before my eyes
      My heart saw your heart smiling
      And never let go

124 Surrounded by blocks
      The quilt-like ones that built you
      I see you now, whole.

125 I can't help but miss
      That won'drous unknowing - where
      Illusions trumped truth

126   The heart deep armor
      Built, with pride, to keep THEM out
      Was woefully stuck

127   What act of Goddess
      Will it take to break the glass
      Caging old heartache

128   Pretend to forget
      What we've known, like fingerprints,
      Since we were children

129   Truth rivers for eyes
      We plunge deep, clothes forgotten
      And lies dripping. Gone.

130   Our messy affair
      And Love – sticky, gooey, mud
      With which we make pie

131   We caught the sunrise
      Fell into sandy blankets
      Swapped new day wishes

132 Remember when we
   Let go even deeper we
   Bulldozed those walls. We.

133 This morning I thought
   I smelled your dirty feet smell
   It was just wishing

134 The cold quips, curses
   Created in your stunned stare –
   Punishment enough

135 If I reach my arms
   Until they hurt from stretching
   Then would I feel you?

136 Passion's renewal
   A forgotten zest for life
   Sparked by conflict

137 Once upon a time
   I left you far behind me
   And you've never gone

Love.Self.Care

138 "Great Hair Day"
    Ease back in the chair
    Soaking in the sweetest Dish
    As locks turn luscious

139 What could be better
    Than a weekend siesta
    And a long, hot bath…

140 Who needs therapy
    When I can throw my head back,
    Open heart, and LAUGH!!!

141 The comforts of home
    Raging fire, cozy chair, love…
    And animal hair

142 In twilight stillness
    Furry friends keep toes toasty
    Simple Fuzzy Love

143 It's the simple things -
Full moons, homemade quilts, good food-
That make life worth it.

144 "Sea Water Solution"
Maritime surgeons
Methodically extract life's
Extrinsic debris

145 Data overload
Rebooting the system
And emptying the trash

146 Even with eyes closed
I can see my jagged edge
And choose to love it

147 Who holds the holder
Whose arms are weary with hope
And filled with regret

148 Clean room, well made bed
Order helps to calm the head
Clearing out the old

Remembering

149 Is this a mirage?
    Here and gone so fast
    Hanging on before it's past

150 But just yesterday
    It was Barbies, doll and bears
    Grown fast, yet still young

151 Your wild, made up dance
    Donned in mom's old scarves and jewels
    Jerky joints make joy

152 My private fireworks –
    Peeking o'er rooftops and trees –
    Invoke youth-filled awww

153 Building sand castles
    And laughing as the ocean
    Whisks them all away!

154 Post beach comatose
    Pummeled by waves and brown skinned
    We, salty, slog home

155 Arms Eyes Open Wide
    Wearing inside skin outside and
    Swapping Secrets

156 "Something Summer"
    Wafting through windows
    Summer supper's savory scent
    Belly full of joy

157 A cozy porch swing.
    Twenty toes. Arm hair tickling.
    And nowhere to go.

158 I see you old friend
    I'm reaching for you
    Calling your name in my sleep

159 Teardrops from up high
    Juicy and cold on my cheeks
    Now I know you're here

160 "Vacation's End"
    One more balmy night
    To remember what I've known
    Simply breathe…and love

161 I thought I was lost
    But when I opened my eyes
    My feet had found home

162 Watching old mem'ries
    Like faded super 8 flicks
    Running through my mind

163 Old suitcase smell
    Your fedora-like hat, pipe
    And shiny new shoes

164 Though pictures may dull
    The good times still rage on
    High life in reverb

165 After all these years
    Schooling & degrees on walls
    I still look for you

166 When I close my eyes
     I can smell you; feel your hand
     Palming my small face.

167 I sat in that chair
     And rocked myself back to sleep
     The way you used to

168 In truth times I can
     Collage the scraps of my life
     To create perfect

169 Meeting you this way
     Births, bills and lovers later
     Still, I feel childish

170 Funny when old things
     Become new things once again –
     Life keeps us humble.

171 In our Sunday best
     We come for soul fulfillment
     And leave with purpose

172 His sing-song cadence
     And our "Hallelujahs" wooed
     Snowfall from heaven

173 Fearing conflict most
      I never told you my thoughts
      I wish we'd fought more

174 Looking back I think
      It's the raw, messy moments
      I'll remember most

175 Between clouds
      Where sun beams down like carnival slides
      There, I picture you.

176 "Losing It"
      Her mind, an attic
      Full of treasures and one bulb
      Dimming over time

177 Broken Cycles Healed
      And though our moments were brief
      We've parted old friends
      (Thanks for always letting me in)

178 The guards are changing
      Old Faithful's moving on and
      Suddenly I'm lost

Life Lessons

179 No matter how deep
     A hunger or pain it will
     Someday find its end

180 The art of winning
     Start with a quiet desire
     Never surrender

181 Showing up for life.
     Doing what I said I'd do,
     When my bed feels great.

182 I'm sure to say "yes"
     To whatever comes my way —
     Leaving "how" behind.

183 Why mend a mistake
     When answers always spring forth
     From a fine-tuned mess

184   Sometimes five minutes
      Is all I need to find the
      Way back to my heart

185   Anticipation
      That trickster who distracts us
      From beautiful now

186   When a simple meal
      Leaves me howling at the moon
      I'll come back for more

187   A once great mountain
      Slowly chipped away - relieved
      Now has disappeared

188   The blurred line between
      Pleasure and Obligation
      Is found in structure

189   How many hours lost
      Waiting for recognition
      From my greatest fans

190   It is possible
      That I don't have the answers
      For anyone else

191   Before my "smart" phone
      Awkward moments in a crowd
      Meant making new friends

192   Fear and Apathy
      Seep through airwaves into me
      Poisonous cocktail

193   It takes some courage
      To achieve the big dreams,
      But more to enjoy them

194   With each passing day
      There's more proof that life's lil kinks
      Don't need ironing

195   The worst kept secret
      Is the one, never spoken,
      That everyone knows

196   Thought I hated war
      But the battles within me
      Could topple empires

197   Mistakes will be made
      But a life moved by passion
      Leads to happiness

198   When life confronts me
      With violent reality
      I respond with love

199   When I dared let go
      I found possibility
      Beyond all I've known

200   Challenges
      Today will soon be
      Laughable

201   The greatest battles
      Live in the silence before
      Quiet, Mirrored, Truth

202 I'm never poised for
      The push into Big Girl Shoes…
      But they always fit

203 Professor Hindsight
      Turns what I once criticized
      To butterfly stuff

204 Brilliance is knowing
      When to push a bit harder
      Or sit back and ride

205 Beneath ambition
      Lies the kernel of a dream –
      My truth and compass

206 Someone's Leap of Faith
      Can launch me across a pit
      Of ineptitude

207 Both joy and grief can
      Persuade the staunchest of foes
      To break bread as one

208 When the listener
Needs an ear, where will she turn?
Run down stones crumble

209 The sweetest revenge
Like too many treats, leaves me sick –
Riddled with grief

210 Divinity
Shines in through the smallest spaces
No need to perform

211 Secrets never told
Snake through family trees
And, like fireworks, explode

212 I trust. I trust. I
Honestly do. That what you
Give comes back to you.

213 I am grateful for
Closed doors as much as for those
That swing wide open

214 When inspiration
    Seems to be just out of reach
    Grab something closer

215 In an instant
    The option least expected
    Can change everything

216 Celestial tugboats
    Lead with vision far beyond
    The scope of our eyes

217 Practice compassion.
    Especially for those folks
    Who just piss you off.

218 Lurking inside me
    Are lovers, clowns & villains –
    Which am I choosing?

219 The bigger life gets
    The more vintage rabbit holes
    Appear on my path

220 When I dare glance back
     I find the tiny steps were
     Truly giant's strides

221 What's been done before
     What feels safe and more secure
     May not be what's right

222 The more I don't know
     The more truth my heart takes in
     The more I let go

223 Racing through lifetimes
     While enlightenment just waits
     For the search to end

224 Mediocrity
     Go with the flow, status quo
     Sometimes that's the key

225 Grow with the flowing
     Let go of "must be" knowing
     Tortoise to the end

226 In every moment
For better & worse – things change
There's comfort in that

227 Think back to child's brain
People were just people then
And they still are.

228 There are some moments
When it truly is hard work
To mind your manners
And there are some folks
Who, like a good paper cut,
Simply will not go

229 Is it perfection?
No. Some miles from it, in fact.
But it's all I've got.

Friends, Family, Home

230 I'm not meant to see
       The dimples in my behind
       That's what friends are for

231 By loving others
       I've discovered how deeply
       I can love myself

232 Once alone I find
       The Krinkle Buzzzzz POP of friends
       Is what makes life sweet

233 Nothing like dear friends
       To remind you that you have
       Everything you need

234 Words cannot express
       The depth of my gratitude
       For this luscious life!

235 Inspired as always
     After we speak I float back
     Into human skin
     Wholly savoring
     Inspiration, Vision, Joy
     The essence of You

236 The success of friends
     Serves as a breathtaking glimpse
     At what dreams will come

237 I always find home
     Safely embraced by friend's arms
     And voices I love

238 Through thick and through thin
     Your voicemail has always been
     A great listener

239 Unlikely friends met
     Miles away from their true shores
     Laughter razes walls

240 If I had to choose
     Gin wins over solitaire
     Each and every time

241 Pedestal returned,
I'm slowly learning to love
Your humanity

242 Enveloped by couch
We laugh. Cry. Plans forgotten
Hours fly like seconds

243 Through murky water
Shines healing light
Rekindled by a family's love

244 With your love you have
Manufactured miracles
And given him hope

245 It's not sanity
That grows from my family tree
We breed crazy fruit

246 From palm trees to snow –
Comforted by warm love hugs
And the smell of home

Joy & The Real Deal

247   "!!!!!!!"
      Exclamation Point!!!
      Do I yell this much in life????!!!!!!
      If so, sedate me.......!!!!!!!!!!!!

248   "Things I've Learned From Toddlers":
      When someone falls down
      It is not polite to laugh
      But sometimes you must

249   The instant headaches
      The twitches in strange places
      How I love caffeine

250   Slurp, smack, crunch and munch
      I can't help but cringe as you
      Gobble down your lunch!

251 Funny how karma
      Seems of greater importance
      When I'm being good

252 There's nothing like a
      Department store fluorescent
      To zap you Mojo

253 Though the lines are drawn
      No two-steppers groove the same
      Honky-Tonk Couture

254 We, the broken ones
      We, who trip over feet to find feet
      Together

255 There's that sweet moment
      When the dawn begins to break
      And you're still dancing

256 Poor little footsie.
      Who shoved you into small shoes
      And ran about town?

257 The thrill of high speeds
      Video game curves, and me,
      Feline at the wheel

258 When my coolness fades
      I unleash some gnarly tunes
      And walk my rock star!

259 Smooth talkin' seventh
      Inverts my afternoon and
      Sends me home again

260 Got a tummy ache
      Dinner was too creative
      Now I pay the price

261 Tie-Dye genie pants
      Transform the night into a
      PJ Fiesta!

262 Tiny beads of sweat
      Snaking their way down my back
      A classy parade

263   If there's such a thing
      As the right road to travel
      This cannot be it

264   My ears are ringing
      From the constant echoing
      Of my neurosis.

265   One day I awoke
      And the wishes of my youth
      Were the facts of my life

266   I often find more wit
      Surrounded by the insane
      Than at fancy meals

267   I've slipped back into
      Comfortable unconsciousness
      And I can't wake up

268   Thanksgiving Trepidation:
      Though vegan herself,
      She knew tryptophan comas
      Could be contagious.

JOY & THE REAL DEAL

269 In my most devlish
   Moments I secretly wish
   Someone would catch me

270 As a child I drew
   But adulthood has taught me
   To play in the gray.

271 Sometimes I wonder
   If in my sleep I live the
   Lives my heart conceives.

272 When your blood's boilin'
   Find out who's holding the match
   And blow that &@*# out

273 Yogi man in white
   I don't know what we just did
   But I feel awesome.

274 "Desert Flower"
   Brilliant, blinding lights
   Endless days and cigarettes
   Who's running this show?

275 Your rhythmic patter
     Leaves me tapping through swing clubs
     And humdrum streets

276 Judy Garland Night
     Cozy Couch, "Girl Crazy" and
     Cocktails with the boys!

277 Your rude retort
     Made my arm hair stand on end
     And then I laughed. Hard.

Spark of Creation –
An Artist's Dilemma

278   To make time for play!
　　　When weary bones turn funny,
　　　Then work truly soars.

279   Walking the thin line
　　　Between cruel obsession and
　　　Gentle readiness

280   There is a pure self
　　　Born out of creating art
　　　Divinely endowed

281   A small, focused group
　　　Will always create something
　　　Larger than they'd planned

282   But to the rambler
　　　His nonsense. Napkin novels.
　　　Became his lifeboats.

283   Today I'm crafting
      Stories for the book I'll write
      When I'm 100.

284   Bleary eyed & pleased
      When the work is good
      Fatigue feels like a reward

285   Beautiful unknown
      Rich with possibility
      Free of fear-filled me

286   But you must create
      For we who live in boxes
      Will die without light

287   Ideas are like kids
      They're made to grow - so catch them
      Quick! Before they go.

288   From the most grand stage
      To an old drafty basement
      Artists are the same

289 Out crept the old troll
　　 Jaundiced from hoarding dead dreams
　　 I fled for my joy

290 Beneath conforming
　　 Lay a corroded trove of
　　 Stifled creations

291 Fatigue bleeding in
　　 Oozing through doubt's well worn grooves
　　 Drip drop on heart's art

292 Speak chant sing, voice
　　 In a tone that's only yours
　　 And we will listen

293 Without distraction
　　 Boredom is redirected
　　 To innovation

294 Hello blank canvas
　　 Taunting me/Enticing me
　　 Daring me to play

295 Illumination
     Finds its way through smog and grit
     Making messy art

296 When vision smashes
     Through sensibility's walls
     You're getting closer…

297 This Artist's Hustle
     Invigorates, Elevates,
     Sets My Spirit Free

298 Upon a bare wall
     I throw my innermost self
     Hoping something sticks

299 Six second fade up -
     The strings begin, wigs pinned tight –
     We all slip away

300 Like well worn blues jeans
     I slip into an old song
     Undone by known strains

301 For one moment of
Still, silent release after
Gifting all my self

302 It takes one great muse
To inspire art, angst and hope
That lasts a lifetime

303 With shredded morale
We crawled past failure's doorway
Toward neighboring success

304 Something must be said.
Gut rumbles. Heart beats. Conscience.
Whispers, "Yes, it's you".

Letting Go

304   To those in despair
　　　Trust fall into open arms:
　　　We long to hold you

305   To combat my fear
　　　I peer into the unknown
　　　And step anyway

306   Beauty's not for keeps.
　　　We indulge with hopeful hearts,
　　　Weeping as it goes.

307   And we won't look 'way
　　　Set sun, shoot star, smile now fade
　　　We will, grateful, watch

308   Waking up to find
　　　Baby booties turned to specs
　　　And parents turned kids

309   Thing about ledges
　　　Is that more often than not
　　　They're just three feet high

310 My floor is sloping.
     Just the smallest bit.
     Yet I still fear falling glass.

311 With an open heart
     I softly whisper "Goodbye"
     To some antique loves

312 Brown bruised arms spread wide
     Free falling into darkness
     Trusting in your sun

313 Though I may feel lost
     I'm going to keep stepping
     And see where I land

314 "Ah, fair" the old man sighed,
     "I used to want that, too."
     Then he smiled and died.

315 "Leap"
     Chasm of mys'try
     New day possibility
     No Contingency

316 Our man was found dead
      We cried and danced til mourn
      Gone, our petty row

317 The long lost father
      Strong, unsure, doing his best
      I see you, my friend

318 Quieted by hope
      We allow some cautious joy
      In the wake of our pain

319 Beneath resentment
      Sits a pool of forgiveness
      Thaw, crack, overflow

320 When the rain began
      I'd long lost myself to the sea
      The storm forgotten

321 Self cracked whip hits
      A frozen taskmaster. Then breath comes
      And the day unfolds

322 There's no balm that soothes
     A wound that's not yours to heal
     So we trust…and wait.

323 Heart connects with heart
     And tension, built up for years
     Dissolves in laughter

334 Can you stomach it?
     Will you dare accept the gift
     Of an answered prayer?

335 When the whisper comes
     I'll listen and, open-armed,
     Run into my life

336 On days like this one
     The tears stay staining my face
     I've stopped asking why

334 And in an instant
     Crucial and foolish matters
     Meant nothing at all

335   If this were the day
       You chose to release all fear
       What would it look like?

336   From defrosting ground
       As buds burst from barren trees
       I fly towards sunshine

337   What could be more grave
       Than the possibility
       Of mere normalcy?

338   Everything is green.
       Unexpected encounters
       Yield hope and fresh eyes.

Ode

339 "9/11"
   Only memories
   Of a city devoted
   To healing itself

340 While I run from rain
   You crouch, dodging stray bullets.
   Wish I could send rain.

341 All you who rally
   For peace in your chosen haunts
   Look like my brothers

342 "Trevon"
   Hooded we now stand
   Challenging brutal silence
   Demanding justice

343 To all you drifters
      Whose passions fill suitcases
      Whose visions stir us

344 "Lilia"
      The day you were born
      Was like a supernova
      Whose brilliance won't fade

345 "Etta"
      Blues-Bird fly 'way home
      Shock of white hair, light skies now
      At Last you fly free

346 "Katrina and…"
      All you Southern Sprites
      Feet planted like ancient trees
      Your faith anchors us

Prayer

347 May we know our worth
　　　When lies outside pose as truth
　　　May we know our worth

348 To be full of life -
　　　Not what would, could, should, will, has,
　　　But the sweet right now.

349 I trust you to know
　　　When we should be joined in love
　　　And dance through your life

350 "Parenthood"
　　　I can only hope
　　　To hold fast when you need love
　　　And then to let go

351 Grow the storage space
    That this heart can be grateful
    For what's mine and yours

352 Be still and un-damn
    This day's hopes, fears and missteps
    May sleep tame wild thoughts

Good Night

353 As schoolgirls jump rope
      I muster an hour's more work
      Longing for twilight

354 One more nibble
      Avoid the soul sucking drivel
      Of doing dishes

355 Tucked inside my bed
      Eavesdropping on nightlife's din
      With a content smile

356 Contemplating life
      In the middle of the night
      Is a sleepless game

357 For once the night falls
      I find my keen self rendered
      Utterly inept

358   Eyes heavy with sleep
      Me, unable to oblige
      Trolling for the zzzzzzzzzzzzzzzz

359   Oh you rattling brain
      These puzzles aren't yours to solve
      So rest now…goodnight

260   Clinging to the night
      Out of fear that tomorrow
      I'll have lost this joy

361   Blessed 3am
      When insomnia meets God
      And sits down for tea

362   Lying still in bed
      The cloud's bird's breath's opus
      Rocks me back to sleep

363   This weary body
      Surrenders to cotton blend
      Enveloped by dream-thoughts

364   Her opiate hum
       Ocean just steps from our sleep
       As we're lulled to peace

365   Surrendered to peace
       Against a breast's rise and fall
       And herb scented sheets

366   As the day closes
       The faithful sandman guides me
       Into dreamy bliss

Epilogue

Once the words had all been written
Once she had said her piece
The truth became her lullaby
And she drifted off to sleep

Thank Yous and Acknowledgements...

This book would not have been created without the support – both emotionally and financially – of very dear family, friends and fans. To those of you who have nudged me to stretch further continuously over the years, who have read and supported my words, and who gave so generously to my crowdfunding campaign I cannot thank you enough. I am humbled by your love always and send it back to you tenfold.

Jeremiah, Mom, Dad, Aly, Mike, Lilia, Mary, Levi, Big Nate, Abe, Amee, Charles, Sara, Azie, Carrie, Lenelle, Anne, Daryl, Jill, Donna, Marty, Karen, Laura, Phyllis, Roger, A.J., Dave, Breanna, Ricki, Eva, Ann K., Gilbert, Leslie, Lynn, Kristen, Sealexan, Keith & Jill, Brittany, Shakun, Carla C., Sharon, Leigh Ann, Pamela, Nancy, Mary R.

www.ingramcontent.com/pod-product-compliance
Lightning Source LLC
Chambersburg PA
CBHW052108070526
44584CB00017B/2395